Shenandoah

Hullihen Williams Moore

Shenandoah

VIEWS OF OUR NATIONAL PARK

University of Virginia Press ❧ Charlottesville & London

For Nancy Harrison Delano Moore

University of Virginia Press
© 2003 Hullihen Williams Moore
All rights reserved
Printed in China on acid-free paper
First published 2003

9 8 7 6 5 4 3 2 1

Library of Congress Cataloging-in-Publication Data

Moore, Hullihen Williams, 1942–
    Shenandoah : views of our national park / Hullihen Williams
Moore.
        p.   cm.
Includes bibliographical references.
    ISBN 0-8139-2224-0 (cloth : alk. paper)—ISBN 0-8139-2225-9
(limited edition cloth : alk. paper)—ISBN 0-8139-2226-7 (pbk. :
alk. paper)
        1. Shenandoah National Park (Va.)—Pictorial works.
2. Shenandoah National Park (Va.)—Description and travel.
3. Shenandoah National Park (Va.)—History. 4. Natural history—
Virginia—Shenandoah National Park. I. Title.
F232.S48M66   2003
917.55'9'00222—dc21   2003007374

Frontispiece: Appalachian Trail and Mist, 1994

Contents

Nevermore, however weary, should one
faint by the way who gains the blessings of one
mountain day; whatever his fate, long life,
short life, stormy or calm, he is rich forever.

JOHN MUIR, June 23, 1869,
My First Summer in the Sierra

MOUNTAIN DAYS

A MATURE DOE BROWSES among fresh green shoots at the edge of a large, grassy meadow dotted with occasional oaks. The morning air is cool, the sky clear, and a light easterly wind blows toward the meadow from the nearby forest. The doe cocks her head, thinking she hears more than the breeze. She raises her nose but senses no danger.

Seventy feet away, a boy hides motionless in the grass. He knows the wind is in his favor; only noise or sudden movement will reveal him. Soon the doe lowers her head and returns to the tender spring grass.

The boy stirs and rises slowly, almost imperceptibly. He leans on one knee for stability, moves his arms up, and focuses directly on the doe. Nothing else exists for him. The doe turns, unconcerned, the dark pines beyond her lightening her dusky brown coat. She raises her head again but still senses nothing unusual.

The boy, who has followed the deer for almost an hour, checks his quarry, then shoots. The click of the shutter startles the deer. She shies a few feet away, then stops and looks back. The boy, Austin, stands, turns, and smiles at me. He knows he has a good picture, and I do, too. We have come to the mountains, and Shenandoah has welcomed us.

Here at Big Meadows, in the center of the Shenandoah National Park, deer are almost always abundant. In late May and early June, when the new fawns arrive, I plan to return with all three of my grandchildren—Austin, his younger brother, Kiernan, and their new brother, Iain Thorn. Together, we will all see new life at Shenandoah.

Ten miles north of Big Meadows stands Stony Man Mountain. Its western crest looks like a silhouette: Stony Man appears to be resting his head on a mountain pillow. When my son, Frank, was ten, as Austin is now, we climbed the trail to the top of Stony Man. As we scrambled onto the rocks where the mountain falls away, the full expanse of the Shenandoah Valley lay before us, with Massanutten Mountain beyond and the Alleghenies in the distance.

We fell silent at the sight. Then we watched a raven circle below, riding the strong updrafts of the mountain's western slope. He rarely flapped his wings yet soon rose level with the mountaintop. He circled more widely. Then he glided over us. We could hear the wind on his black wings.

Our long silence, a kind of reverence, gave way to talk of rocks and birds. I balanced my camera on a large stone to catch the vista of sky, clouds, rocks, valley, and mountains. Then I set the timer and ran to kneel beside Frank before the shutter snapped. Frank is a man now; the colors in that picture have faded, but the memory remains.

When I climbed Stony Man again recently, Austin climbed it with me. As we looked across the valley from the stone forehead, I noticed that the words for wonder have changed in twenty years, but the reaction remains the same, for me and for young Austin as well. Again, we looked and listened. Again I balanced my camera and ran to join the picture. I never tire of that walk and that view, and now I have more children to walk and look and listen with me, more of them to wait while I join the picture on this mountain.

My memories of Shenandoah National Park are even clearer in my mind than the images in this book. In addition to Austin stalking his deer and my climbs up Stony Man, I still smile when I recall my son, Frank, counting deer from the car as we drove along the Skyline Drive at dusk. I smile again when I think of his expression the moment he realized we might be counting the same deer twice as we returned to the lodge. And I remember my daughter Sara's trips as well. She walked atop the low stone walls at each overlook and sat astride a pony that I led in circles near the stables at Big Meadows. But mostly she enjoyed the solitude as I do now, curled up looking and reading.

For me, this park holds more than fond memories, childhood adventures, and deer too numerous to count. Wonder, beauty, wildness, and peace live here. The park offers solitude so deep that the visitor can be one with the earth. And at Shenandoah each season is special. Each has gifts for those who go and watch and listen.

Winter can be peaceful, a time to walk the trails alone. The air is crisp and clear, the views at their best. Long vistas show through the bare trees; the Massanutten and the distant ridges of the Appalachians and the Alleghenies appear clearer and closer. The silver stones of Old Rag Mountain gleam from afar. The clouds, too, are different. On clear winter days, fleeting clouds are crisp against a sky that appears to be a darker blue.

It is 7:00 a.m. Light snow falls from a gray January sky. I am the park's first visitor of the day. The roads are white under packed dry snow from the day before; tracks are barely visible. The Skyline Drive is closed, but the road into Sugar Hollow to the North Fork of the Moormans River is passable. No tracks but my own mark the walk to the river. The day is glorious, twenty degrees and windless. Snow falls straight down. I see no deer; not a squirrel, a mouse, or even a bird stirs. The animals are in seclusion. My boots, crunching in the dry, soft snow, and my breathing are the only sounds. The icy air and my heartbeat are the only sensations. Each step disturbs the scene. There is no touching branch or rock. On each, tiny flakes have gently stacked themselves. All rocks are rounded now, each jagged edge smoothed by mounded snow.

I am an intruder, as anything that moves or changes this scene must be. I step slowly and deliberately, not because the walk is difficult, but because I stop to hold my breath and look and listen. Above the sound of my heartbeat, I hear the river murmuring quietly, low water in winter, muffled by snow. I walk, stand, watch, and listen. I do not feel the cold or mark the passing time. The water moves gently, darkened by the riverbed, a strong contrast to white rocks and branches.

The snow slows, then stops, but the air remains still. Then birds appear, flitting from limb to limb, occasionally dislodging snow, returning me to a more familiar reality. But the trackless and solitary path was just as real.

The view up the narrow river reminds me that I have my camera. As the river curves away under the arches of snow-covered trunks and limbs, it disappears under a pine. The shapes and tones of the rocks and snow and water in winter light are intriguing. I step out of nature and start to analyze, preparing for a picture. The beauty remains, but the magic becomes a memory. I make only two images, and even so I must trample the snow to find the best view. The next traveler will see my intrusion.

Snow remakes the winter landscape; ice reshapes it into strange, beautiful structures. Trees wear glassy jackets and glisten in the morning light, while streams, falls, and cascades build sculptures from fine spray in frigid air. As the wet rock freezes, the spray builds upon it, freezing drop by drop, until ice curves over the water. The frozen canopy takes shape, as more spray falls, freezing on contact.

Where water is plentiful, ice may build on a fallen log or convenient stone to create a backdrop for a waterfall, a curtain whose pleats are icicles as high as the falls, molded together by spray, air, and sun. Because the water moves, pools at the base of such falls rarely freeze. Instead, ice creeps out from the pools' sides in a white, scalloped edge.

The streams that feed Naked Creek Falls are narrow, often only a foot wide or less. Spray from the streams' cascades creates a miniature sculpture garden. What appears from a distance to be an arch across the stream is icy lace, thin and delicate as a handkerchief. The lace lies thick and close to the bank at the cascade's base, becoming finer and more detailed as it climbs up and out. The sun highlights each stitch.

On the opposite bank, weather and water produce not lace but a crystal orb as round and clear as any created for the czar. The bank embraces the sphere; as water and cold air swell the crystal, delicate lines of decoration appear. Downstream from the lace and orb, grasses and plant stems hanging from the bank help form other wonders for the sculpture garden.

Only on the cusp of the season, and then very rarely, a thick, white, water-laden mist may settle on the mountains to create hoarfrost. Tiny crystals freeze to every branch, twig, and blade of grass, sometimes adding an inchwide ribbon along the sides of limbs. The frost transforms the forest, making each tree, plant, and shrub visible in a new way. Viewed from another ridge, the mist rises to reveal the frost line on the trees, dark and gray below and white above.

Even a single tree coated in hoarfrost is a spectacular and delicate marvel. A heavily covered roadside pine at Big Meadows ceases being a pine or even a tree. Hoarfrost turns the needles into flowers that weigh the branches down. Crystals outline the dark trunk and whiten the grass below the tree. Frost, not snow, has painted every blade.

The large and magnificent tree I call Big Meadows Oak also wears white, rising high above its young. The mist soon ascends and the sky clears, and for the few moments before the frost falls, the grand tree stands against a deep blue sky, every inch adorned with brilliance.

Spring comes slowly to the park. When willows in the valley turn pale green in late winter or early spring, the mountain ridges sleep. The piedmont and valley come to life as their trees bud and leaf. The maple's new growth and seeds burst red and the grass springs green. Trees at the mountains' feet begin to unfurl tiny leaves that green and grow. Then spring starts up the mountains, climbing them at one hundred feet a day. The line is not always straight, because some species leaf earlier than others. But the burgeoning marches upward.

Meanwhile, at the mountains' crests, winter reigns. The oaks, among the last to leaf, are tight, although their branch tips have begun swelling; last year's leaves have only recently finished falling. These crisp, curled oak leaves show that spring is near, even though the forest floor looks sodden and lifeless, much as it did in February and early March.

The stem of the bloodroot rises, sometimes even before the last winter storm, another sign that spring will soon move into the mountains. Even in bloom, the bloodroot's leaves remain curled around the stalk at first, as if seeking protection. Its flowers, white petals with a yellow center, are among the harbingers of a Shenandoah spring.

As spring advances, other wildflowers show themselves. On springtime mountain days, I can walk among wild geranium and watch the bells of columbine dance in the wind. Trillium blooms, covering entire hillsides in pink and white. May brings the pink lady's slipper. A single pink orchid rises from each plant, while its leaves remain close to the ground. The yellow lady's slipper blooms from May until June. This orchid grows in bunches, and each plant has several blooms. Mayapples, too, rise beside the road in their month, each plant's leaves spreading to shelter the single white flower below. Then, in June, the Robertson Mountain trail to Old Rag Mountain passes through a tunnel of pink and white mountain laurel.

Ferns shoot forth in spring, too. Beside my feet, two fiddleheads have turned aside crisp oak leaves. Two pale-green stalks, glistening with dew and topped by white-green heads ready to unfurl, face each other. A third frond, almost white, coils tight and low between them. Now the oak leaves dwarf the fern's emerging shoots, but soon the new fern will take its first breath, convert light to energy, and rise above the forest floor. Nearby ferns have already begun uncoiling their pale-green fronds. Others remain still curled, hiding their tender tips.

Spring fills Shenandoah's falls and streams. These mountain falls and quick clear waters will revive visitors dulled by winter in the city. Bright light and deep shadows move across the water from morning to late afternoon. Shadow and light crisscross the rivers and streams as wind moves through new leaves.

Dusk on a spring day is a special time to visit rivers and streams. As the light starts to fade in Sugar Hollow, I walk up the North Fork of the Moormans River, not far from where I spent that January day in untouched snow. The wind, as usual, dies before evening. As I look up the river to where the Moormans bends before a large poplar, a shoulder-high boulder stands at my right. Newly leafed limbs reach out and down toward the river's center. The light, too, is quiet, an enveloping presence that brings out the detail in the dense woods on my left.

The shifting shadows from sun and wind are gone; the shape and currents of the river are clear. The flowing waters outline the rocks above the surface and mark the ones below. At dusk, the water seems to quiet and collect itself, a moving cloth that runs smooth, curves gently around rocks, and mounds up to cover the stones beneath the surface. I have walked this river often. I know just the place to make a picture. The weather, the water, and the light support me, and I make a long exposure that captures the water as one element, flowing and connected to all around it. The leaves are so still that their detail is clear, another touch of richness in the scene.

A few weeks after that picture, a flood hit Sugar Hollow. Continuous soaking rain liquefied the ground. Hillsides collapsed in a chaos of huge trees, mud, and rocks and crashed down to the river's edge. Rains continued to swell the Moormans. Great old trees along the river fell, and immense boulders moved. The rising water swept most of the trees a mile away or more, and moving rocks stripped the bark from the few trees lodged in the riverbed.

In less than a day, this stretch of river changed forever, snapping trees one hundred feet tall and two feet in diameter like pencils. The flood remade the entire landscape, moving the river itself seventy to one hundred feet away from where it flowed that May evening when I made the picture. The water carried boulders the size of automobiles downriver to the reservoir. The water left expanses of hundreds of feet treeless. Where an arch of branches once stretched over the river, a field of stones baked in the sun.

When I returned to that place, using landmarks from above the flood, the shoulder-high boulder, like the trees, was gone. A quiet stream now wandered through an empty field of raw stones and rocks. Smaller stones cluttered the edges where the flood's rush was slower. In the center, where the flood was strongest, lay larger stones and boulders. Giant sycamores had vanished, leaving bare roots and fragments of trunks, foundations that had lain safely underground for years until the deluge.

Change had come to Shenandoah, but not catastrophe. Within months, pioneer plants sprang up in the rich soil the flood deposited among the rocks. New life and landscape have replaced the old, although it will be centuries before the scene looks again as it did that May.

Spring recalls other lives as well. Each year in this season I walk along the fire road near Jarmans Gap. A wall near the stream tells of a home place once nearby. Across the road, foundation corners and fifteen-foot American boxwoods rise above the grass. A family once lived here, a family forced from this home to make way for the park in the 1930s. After the home was razed, nature took over once more. Nameless now, that family built and planted well. The wall near the road, neglected for decades, still stands. The boxwoods thrive. Each spring when I return, the daffodils bloom and bloom, though they have been untended almost seventy years.

Spring also is a good time to visit the park's cemeteries. The living were cast out, but the dead rest undisturbed in more than one hundred cemeteries scattered throughout the park. Some are merely fieldstones grouped near a home's empty foundation. Others, however, contain new stones and recent burials. At the Cave family cemetery, nestled on a sloping mountainside near Fishers Gap, rows of fieldstones, some only inches high, give way to modern markers. Live daffodils, and artificial flowers as well, testify to past and present love and care. At the heart of the Dean cemetery, a magnificent lilac blooms each spring, just as it did before the land became a park. That cemetery is still active; new residents come to join the others every few years.

In June, summer takes over the mountains. The grasses at Big Meadows grow high and green, hiding the new fawns born since mid-May. The new fawns climb upright on wobbly legs almost instantly. By mid-June they follow their mothers to the meadow and curl invisibly in the grass while the does browse. A walk around Big Meadows when summer has finally arrived reveals a dozen or more fawns, hidden near their mothers or standing at the forest's edge behind them.

Summer can be a quiet time in the park. Although there are more visitors than in early spring, Shenandoah welcomes each of us with her many offerings. Even on a crowded day, silence and solitude are always only a short walk away.

The June sun is high. I walk a deer trail at the edge of Big Meadows, as I often have. Two oaks barely six feet apart spread their branches toward the ground. They are stocky; despite two-foot trunks, they rise less than twenty-five feet above the tall, lush grass. When I duck down to enter their shade, the air cools instantly. A light breeze brushes my face. The tall grasses bend under their own weight but do not break; they sway gently. In one place the grass is matted down into an oval, perhaps a fawn's hiding place.

The grass and earth are soft; the stones are far enough apart to make stretching out easy. At first, I have trouble lying still and concentrating on the wind, the silence, and the oak trees. It is hard not to think of city things. Time passes. My muscles ease, and my surroundings come into full focus. Time passes, unnoticed now. Grasses blowing gently against my face startle me. Plans for the rest of the day and some city thoughts return, but I rise refreshed, grateful to be under the oaks at Shenandoah.

As I walk on, Big Meadows Oak draws me to it, as always. It is gnarled and weathered. A copse of descendants, younger and shorter, surrounds it. In more than twenty years of walking here, I have watched this tree grow old. Years ago, in full exuberant leaf with brawny outstretched branches, it towered above its young. Now, some branches are bare and others have fallen at the feet of the young. The young oaks now rise higher on the mother tree. Each time I return to Big Meadows, I wonder if I'll still see the great oak among her young. I fear that I may not. The old tree must be too weak to take many more summer thunderstorms or to bear the weight of many more winters' ice.

Summer quiets the streams and falls, giving them an inviting peace and coolness on hot days. I often walk the Rose River trail to where it meets Hogcamp Branch, then I turn and climb the trail beside the branch. This walk along the water through a high canopy forest is cool and peaceful. I find no roses and never will; the little river is named for early settlers, not flowers. The sixty-seven-foot Rose River Falls enlivens this walk. Usually, and especially in summer, the water flows over the rock rim near the trail and tucks itself among the rocks, leaving the rest of the thirty-foot-wide rock face dry or merely damp.

I once saw this fall booming full. White water poured across the top from every rock and crevice one late summer after an unusual series of long rainfalls. The trailside waterfall overflowed, creating layers of falls that covered up the rocks below. Water rushed along the stones' faces, outlining their cracks, ledges, and fissures. Other streams, forced from the rock wall into the air, hit and bounced, outlining the fall's larger features and covering the interior flows with a gauzy spray. Across the rest of the fall rim, water gushed from every opening, creating a series of falls. I saw this dramatic and beautiful sight just that single time. Only by returning again and again do we receive such gifts.

This summer walk offers other gifts as well. On the climb along Hogcamp Branch after leaving the Rose River, the stream is quiet; wide flat stones cross the creek bed. Where the shade still covers the creek, dozens of cascades, miniature falls, and pools murmur, calling me off the trail after the hot walk up the branch.

Moss-covered ancient logs along the creek stay spring green all summer. The water is always cold; the rocks are comfortable and cool. I sit here and focus on the water, listen only to the water, look only at the water, and feel the outer world fall away. These are wonderful napping rocks.

Summer clouds produce mountains of their own, cumulus mountains. On a hot summer day, these flat-bottomed clouds form just as earth's mountains do, building upon themselves. Their sharp outlines billow out and up, clear against a deep blue sky and often with distinct white-on-white detail. The cloud mountains rise, build, and change. They move away, they disperse, or they gather themselves into a glorious summer thunderstorm. In these mountains, such a storm can be magnificent.

The storm appears across a distant ridge. Hard rain obscures the ridgeline first, then moves down the mountain, across the valley and up toward the observer. The thunder here is different from the sharp claps of the flatland. It rolls around me as the storm approaches, sometimes faint, sometimes strong. The thunder's roll may reverberate for long seconds through the peaks and hollows. Rain announces its movement up the mountain by sight as well as sound. Tree tops bend with wind and water and then disappear as the storm approaches. As it arrives, large, single drops fall hard at first. They darken the rock before me slowly, circle by circle. Then the storm breaks fully, weighting the air with water, wind, and darkness. Terrifying, exhilarating flashes of light and thunder punctuate the deluge, and all human senses know the power of nature, a power that turns us to her, that makes us hear, feel, and see only her.

The storm passes as quickly as it came. The sun returns, catching the raindrops that cover every leaf and flower, every grass and sedge. The grasses at Big Meadows are bent, some even broken, by their weight or by the wind. They sparkle and so does the world. We emerge from such storms refreshed and energized.

Fall's first sign appears in September: a single bright-red oval leaf catches my eye as I walk a trail. That one brilliant leaf on a gum tree is not a sign of illness; gum tree leaves turn early but turn one by one at first. Summer's heat continues, but this red signal says that change is near.

While the gum tree is early and bright, it is not part of the great display for which the park is famous; too few blaze too early, not enough for the postcard colors that bring the crowds. Fall moves down the mountain much less systematically than spring moves up. The trees turn at various times, some losing their leaves well before others. But color is fall's hallmark at Shenandoah. Color draws people up from the flatland to watch as it transforms the mountains.

Fall colors are changing as the dominant species in Shenandoah's forests are changing. Gypsy-moth incursions have made oaks less dominant than a decade ago. Oaks' dusky yellows and reds don't set the mountains or trails ablaze as do the hickories' and poplars' glowing yellows. The poplar is spreading along lower elevations, so yellow will become a stronger element in the park's fall plumage. As the season changes, maples, particularly the red and sugar maples, add their fire, brilliant reds and oranges that, like the hickories' bright yellow, appear to glow.

In October I walk cross-country through one of the park's many hollows at the mountains' feet. Many leaves have fallen, but the hickories and poplars still have color, and the maples are at their height. I seek a homesite whose chimney still stands; I have its coordinates. A twenty-foot chimney should be easy to find. After more than an hour's walk along the creek, I reach a sharp turn and head uphill. Poplars here stand close together; their remaining leaves, bright in the autumn sun, flutter and turn with the wind. Although I must be near, I see no chimney.

Then I realize that the tree trunks and the chimney rocks are the same color. Columns rise everywhere—columns of poplars. As I scan the mountain, yellow surrounds me in the wind, yellow leaves cast shadows across the trees. Walking uphill, I catch one glimpse of orange-red, one flag of difference in the yellow poplar and hickory. This becomes my landmark to keep an eye on as I climb. My decision makes me stumble; I look ahead rather than at the ground and there is no trail. When my foot strikes still another stone, I do look down. It is a foundation-stone.

Twenty feet away, the chimney rises like the poplars. Pieces of a stove and a broken cookpot show that I am inside this house, which was once a home. Broken steps mark the front door. A straggly privet hedge stands in the yard; the ruins behind it must have been the springhouse. Several small, spotted apples still cling to the gnarled branches of two old apple trees; windfalls lie on the ground. The family left this home more than sixty years ago. Since then, poplars have crowded together to fill the yard and garden. Tall, straight, and fast-growing, they surrounded the house; several now grow from within the foundation. An old maple, my orange-red beacon, marks the edge of what was the yard. The newcomers tower over it.

What a place to be born. What a place to grow up. Winters must have been frigid;

food might have been scarce at times. Life must have been hard. But on this fall day, life also must have been wonderful.

The air is warm, not hot. The clearing stretches away; the fall garden grows close by. The apples have been dried on the roof and stored. The potatoes remain to be dug. The family is readying itself for winter. The children play. This, too, was life at Shenandoah. For a time, I can join that life. For a time, I can belong to this house and home.

Fall also brings mist and fog. When the earth still holds enough summer heat to be warmer than the air, mist or fog rises up. When fog forms in the valley, the mountain dweller looks across a white sea. Those islands rising in the sea are mountaintops. As the air warms, fog climbs among the hollows and up the mountains. At still other times, fog or clouds fall on the mountains from above.

The Appalachian Trail follows the park's ridgeline, turning and winding through Shenandoah's forests for more than one hundred miles. White blazes mark the trail. The air is cool, and fog has settled on the mountains as I begin walking this famous trail. I have traveled this section many times, but each time is unique.

The leaves that cover the forest floor and trail are mostly brown, though some still have color. All are curled and crisp; rain, snow, and ice have not soaked and packed them yet. The woods are still leafy and sheltered; young trees arch across the trail before me. No wind blows. Fog lingers in the still air. The forest feels closer, more intimate. Squirrels hustle noisily beside the trail, and leaves crunch underfoot with every step I take.

The mist beckons. As I come close, every feature of the forest becomes clear and sharp. But those farther on, hidden in fog, reveal themselves only as I approach. The trail turns right and disappears into unseen woods. As I follow in the mist, the trail turns before two oaks. One, tall and straight, reaches for the light. The other, larger at the base, has two trunks; perhaps it broke off young and grew anew from the break. The squirrels pause; all is still.

This, too, is the Appalachian Trail. Not simply a beaten track walked by thousands each year from Georgia to Maine, but a place of almost eerie solitude as well. Walking the entire 2,100-mile trail seems too much, like something to conquer instead of a place of discovery. The mist reminds me that I relish this trail a turn at a time.

Years at Shenandoah, mountain days in every season, have brought me the park's blessings and enriched my spirit forever. The images in this book are traces of countless glorious mountain days. I have absorbed these fleeting moments; these amazing days still saturate me. They remain immortal in me, and I share here what I have caught of that immortality.

Views of Our National Park

Baldface Mountain Overlook, 1981

Baldface Mountain Overlook, 1988

Stony Man Mountain, 1995

14 🦌

Dogwoods, 1995

❦ 15

Bloodroot at Sugar Hollow, 1994

New Ferns, 1992

17

Doyles River Falls, 1983

Little Fall and Fern, 1990

Rose River Falls, High Water, 2000

Dancing Dogwoods, 1997

Mountain Stream, 1996

Apple Blossoms and Old Rag, 1995

Service Berry and Dogwood, 1999

Old Rag Mountain, 1982

Young Ferns and Oaks, 2000

🌱 27

ABOVE: Hogcamp Branch, 1987
OPPOSITE: Whiteoak Falls, 1982

28 🦌

Mayapples, Rain, 1996

False Hellebore, 1998

ABOVE: Ice Orb and Lace, 1991

OPPOSITE: Frozen at Naked Creek, 1991

33

Downstream, Moormans River, 1997

Cold Heart, Hogcamp Branch, 1997

Horse Pot, 1996

Silver Leaf, 1992

37

Mountain Clouds, 1999

Big Meadows Oak, Summer Clouds, 1999

Moormans River, Sugar Hollow, Spring, 1995

Board Detail, Cabin Remains, 1996

Seeds, 1990

🌱 43

ABOVE: Flood Tree Remains, Moormans River, 1996
OPPOSITE: Dark Hollow Falls, 1982

ABOVE: Skyline Vista, 1988

OPPOSITE: Flame Cloud, 1988

✿ 47

Forest Floor, Limberlost, 1990

Big Meadows Branch and Grass, 1990

Big Meadows Oak, Spring Frost, 1991

South River Falls, 1987

Old Rag Boulder and View, 2001

Lewis Falls, 1987

Chimney, October Light, 1999

🐾 55

ABOVE: Moormans River, Winter, 1995
OPPOSITE: Overall Run Falls, 2002

ABOVE: Big Meadows Pine, Fog and Ice, 1991
OPPOSITE: Ribbon of Whiteoak, 1982

Ghost Trees, 1996

Ivy Creek Overlook, Clouds, 1990

Rest in Peace, 2000

Cave Family Cemetery, 2000

Winter Frost, Skyline Drive, 1993

65

CREATION *of a* PARK

A SIXTEEN-YEAR-OLD BOY'S first glimpse of Stony Man Mountain more than a century ago may have played a part in the selection of the Shenandoah area as a national park. The boy was George Freeman Pollock, and the year was 1886. Pollock wanted to become a naturalist; his mother helped him secure an unpaid assistantship to the chief taxidermist at the Smithsonian Institution. The boy's duties included occasional specimen-gathering trips to nearby Maryland and Virginia. George's father suggested a place in Virginia worth exploring.

Years earlier, during a brief copper boom in the Virginia mountains, Pollock's father had been an investor in the Miners Lode Copper Company. The mines were never profitable, and the company had abandoned them long ago, although it still owned the land. Mr. Pollock thought George might find interesting specimens on the more than 12,000-acre tract.

Intrigued by his father's suggestion, young George Freeman Pollock set out for Page County, Virginia, in October of 1886. He had scant directions, knowing only that the land lay on and around a mountain called Stony Man.

Although he had difficulties reaching the mountain, Pollock remembered his first view of the Blue Ridge and Stony Man fondly. The air was crystal clear, and the panorama of the mountains spread before him like a painting in three dimensions. Later he wrote: "How little did my father know of what he possessed—a veritable paradise on earth!"

Young George Freeman was an entrepreneur and salesman and was soon developing a resort. By 1891, Stony Man Camp, with tents and a single building, was full for the summer. The resort expanded as Pollock cleared trails and a dining hall was built by a private guest. Cabins replaced tents. The bonfires made with leftover stumps gave way to the occasional costume ball.

Pollock continued to develop and protect the resort. His wife, Addie, joined in, saving Limberlost, a nearby forest of 350- and 400-year-old hemlocks, scheduled for logging until she paid $1,000 for the logging rights in 1920. She also loaned George Freeman substantial sums so that he could keep his "camp" operating. Stony Man Camp became Skyland, a large resort that included a recreation hall, a dining hall for 150, and numerous cabins.

Although the idea of a national park in the southern Appalachians had been discussed since the early 1900s, it was not until 1924 that significant action was taken. In February of that year, Secretary of the Interior Hubert Work appointed a five-member committee to determine if there was land in the southern Appalachians suitable for a national park.

Harold Allen, a Washingtonian and a longtime summer resident of Skyland, saw a newspaper article about the committee's search for national park land. He sent the clipping to Pollock with a note: "Why not Skyland?" Before Allen returned to Skyland that summer, he had learned that the committee believed there were no acceptable sites north of the Great Smoky Mountains. Nevertheless, Allen brought along the committee's questionnaire. Pollock, Allen, and George H. Judd, a publisher who was also a summer resident of Skyland, completed it. Then Allen and Judd lobbied in Washington.

Meanwhile, Pollock and his friends joined many others in Virginia who were already seeking to have a national park in the Commonwealth. State leaders, individuals, and organizations, particularly Shenandoah Valley, Inc., lobbied intensively for the Blue Ridge. Finally, Colonel Smith, the special committee's secretary, agreed to encourage the committee to look at Virginia. Besides Skyland and the surrounding Blue Ridge, nearby Massanutten was also proposed for consideration. In addition, dozens of other sites in neighboring states were championed for consideration.

Smith brought one member of the committee to Virginia in September of 1924. Several hundred residents, including a band, met them in Luray. When the visitors had to decide whether to visit Skyland or competing Massanutten first, Pollock persuaded them to see Skyland. A brief inspection was enough to convince the committee representatives to convene the entire committee at Skyland. Now the Blue Ridge had a real chance.

Pollock prepared thoroughly, bringing in extra help to clear new trails and to build towers from which committee members could see the full beauty of the Blue Ridge. Shenandoah Valley, Inc., spent over $10,000 in this effort. When the committee arrived, most members still believed that nothing suitable lay north of the Great Smoky Mountains. After their visit, they changed their minds. Perhaps it was the hemlocks of Limberlost or the cascades of Whiteoak Canyon.

In December 1924 the committee recommended the Blue Ridge area between Front Royal and Waynesboro, including Pollock's Skyland, as a site for an Appalachian national park. To crown the park, the committee proposed a "Skyline Drive" along the ridgeline, offering views of the Shenandoah Valley and the piedmont plain. By 1926 Congress had approved legislation authorizing the establishment of the park, specifying a minimum area of 521,000 acres, and stipulating that the land be acquired at no expense to the federal government. These requirements would prove troublesome for Virginia.

After the act passed, Virginia had two important and interrelated tasks—first, to raise money to buy the land, and second, to acquire clear title to the property. To raise money, the state had to convince its people that the park was a good idea. Besides appealing to the honor of the Commonwealth, park backers stressed economics and preservation.

Brochures promised citizens of the Commonwealth "tangible returns" from increased tourism and described scenery as a "cash crop." Superficial and sometimes unintentionally humorous economic analyses, complete with illustrations, predicted that the park would bring at least $100 million to Virginia every year. One brochure forecast 250,000 new visitors to Virginia annually, tourists at the park who would not otherwise visit. "This is exactly the number that visited Rocky Mountain National Park in 1924," said the brochure, which suggested that the new park should draw even more new visitors because of the demographics of the area. The brochure also included projections based on the quarter-of-a-million new visitors: "If they average ten meals at a dollar a meal . . . if they average three nights in a hotel each, at $22.00 a week . . . if they average three days each, inside Virginia's borders and spend $3.33 a day in retail stores, they will add $2,500,000 to the income from . . . [each] source."

The backers' second point was that the park preserved a natural area within hours of Washington and within a day's ride of forty million visitors, a refuge where those in the city might come to be refreshed. While that goal was, and is, laudable, the literature promoting it was often misleading and filled with exaggeration. Written materials concluded that the park would be no different from those in the West that preserved existing wilderness.

Brochures, some quoting the committee, described the proposed park as a sort of wilderness Eden untouched by man, "an irregular strip of virgin forest sixty-six miles long and from eight to eighteen miles wide." The steep slopes of the mountains have "saved for us through centuries of civilization more than six hundred square miles of almost untouched native forest within ninety miles of the nation's capital." Old Rag Mountain "towers above slopes of virgin forest." Although the brochure acknowledged that some logging had occurred, it described the forests as "an invaluable exhibit of the wilderness that covered eastern North America . . . when our forefathers settled at Jamestown and Plymouth."

The area selected for the park was indeed beautiful, rugged, and wild; it also included virgin forests. The land, however, was not uninhabited, as the brochures suggested. Much of it was settled, and parts were being farmed and logged. Crude roads crisscrossed the mountains, and homes dotted many hollows. Over the years, the land had been divided into many separate parcels. In 1914 the Department of Agriculture reported that fewer than 10,000 acres of virgin timber still stood in the area. A former resident who lived at the base of Old Rag spoke to me of apple orchards, not virgin forests.

Literature promoting the park also sometimes took a competitive, hectoring tone. Rather than simply extolling the beauty of the Blue Ridge's soft curves, it compared the mountains to the Rockies and Yosemite: "It is important to realize that far too much is made of altitude in comparing our eastern and western mountains. The Rockies, rising to twelve thousand feet from valleys nine thousand feet in altitude, or the Blue Ridge rising to four thousand feet from valleys less than a thousand feet in altitude—what difference in size to the observer? Stony Man in the Blue Ridge towers above Shenandoah as high as El Capitan above Yosemite."

The push to create Shenandoah National Park ignored much of what makes this park unique, both the good and bad. It took years for the government to understand the park as a living laboratory, an experiment in the forest's ability to rejuvenate itself. Only recently has the Park Service acknowledged and discussed publicly the pain and tragedy caused by Virginia's forcible removal of residents and destruction of their homes.

Park supporters and state officials originally estimated the property's cost at $2.5 million, assuming 400,000 acres at $6 per acre. By late spring of 1926, when President Calvin Coolidge signed the bill providing for a minimum size of 521,000 acres, only $1.2 million had been pledged. By August of 1927, it was clear that estimates were low and the cost of land would exceed $6 million.

In 1928 Congress reduced the minimum acreage to 321,000, and the Virginia General Assembly appropriated $1.25 million to acquire land. Even then, the project's future was unclear. William Carson, director of the Virginia Commission on Conservation and Development, was the park's fundraiser. After the 1928 election, Carson urged the new president, Herbert Hoover, to locate a "summer White House" in the park area.

Hoover agreed, paying personally for the rustic Rapidan Camp that remains in the park today. Carson, meanwhile, arranged fishing rights and road improvements for the area. News of the president's retreat helped give the area visibility, especially during Hoover's 1929 conference there with British prime minister Ramsay MacDonald.

Although Franklin D. Roosevelt is rightly credited with most of the public works that developed Shenandoah National Park, the Hoover administration used federal funds and local workers in 1931 to build a road from Rapidan Camp to Skyland and farther north to Route 211 at Thornton Gap. By then, however, the Great Depression had dried up private funding and forced another reduction of the minimum size of the park to 160,000 acres in 1932.

Meanwhile, Virginia needed to acquire the property. Boundaries and titles were unclear, many owners and residents did not want to sell or move, and individual condemnation suits were costly, time consuming, and difficult to prosecute. The state eventually would take 1,088 tracts, affecting both landowners and more than 450 residents.

William Carson asked for advice from his older brother, who had served on the Supreme Court of the Philippines. The older Carson outlined blanket condemnation laws that allowed the government of the Philippines to seize the land of religious orders and transfer them to Filipino peasants. William Carson prepared similar legislation allowing Virginia to file a single suit in each county condemning land for the park. Thousands of suits became only eight.

The Depression, meanwhile, had ruined property values. Augusta County may provide an extreme example: there, thirty-nine tracts, totaling more than 11,000 acres, were valued for condemnation at an average of $1.68 per acre. Interestingly, George Freeman Pollock's land was mostly appraised at $1.00 an acre; he received less than $30,000 for Skyland and over 12,000 acres in Page, Madison, and Rappahanock Counties. Residents who did not own the land were entitled to little; they were, however, paid for the improvements on the property. Those who could and did sell received assurances that they could continue living on the land based on the Hoover administration's policy.

In February of 1934, under the Franklin Roosevelt administration, the National Park Service announced that all residents would have to vacate before the federal government accepted lands for the park. Virginia officials and citizens alike protested the reversal of the Hoover policy. Secretary of the Interior Harold Ickes, however, supported removal. The federal government later relented, allowing some older residents to live out their lives in the park. By 1940 only seventy-eight remained in the park; the last resident died in 1979.

Because the evicted often returned to their homes or moved into a nearby cabin, homes and buildings were destroyed as residents were removed. Sometimes, homes were dismantled and the materials were then used to build outbuildings for resettlement communities outside the park. Programs eventually were developed to help the displaced, and the Resettlement Administration established seven communities near the park, where families could buy homes. Those who could meet the government's economic viability criteria could move into the communities with no down payment and a thirty-year low-interest loan.

In 1933 young men in Roosevelt's newly created Civilian Conservation Corps (CCC) began moving into the park. They blazed trails, fought fires, and graded and planted washed-out areas. This was the first time away from home and the first job for many in an era when food, shelter, and a job were scarce. At the height of the CCC, almost a thousand of these young men worked in the park. They lived in six camps inside the park and four beyond the park boundary. CCC work in the park continued until the outbreak of World War II. Signs throughout the park now tell the locations of some of the camps.

In 1935 picnic grounds at Pinnacles and South River opened, and finally, on December 26, 1935, Secretary of the Interior Harold Ickes accepted deeds from the Commonwealth of Virginia conveying 176,429 acres to the federal government. The Shenandoah National Park was officially established. On July 3, 1936, President Roosevelt dedicated the park. The north section of the Skyline Drive opened in October, and three years later, in August 1939, the final section opened.

By 1937 over one million had visited the Shenandoah National Park; by 1939 it had received more visitors than any other national park. Ironically, the questionable estimates in brochures a decade earlier proved too low. Today, almost 1.7 million visitors come to the park annually, more than six times the optimistic estimates of park supporters.

COMPARED TO MORE FAMOUS western parks like Yellowstone (designated a national reservation in 1872) and Yosemite (made a national park in 1890), Shenandoah is a young park. But geologically it is far older: its history takes place over the grandest blocks of time. Unlike the sharp young western peaks, mere tens of millions of years old, the core stone of the park's mountains is more than one billion years old. These mountains, the Blue Ridge, are part of the Appalachians, stretching from Canada to Alabama.

Just east of the Blue Ridge, Old Rag Mountain rises alone above the hills of the piedmont. The park's boundary extends away from the ridgeline to include this solitary peak. The mountain's stone, called, appropriately, Old Rag Granite, crystallized more than a billion years ago from molten magma deep in the earth.

The earth's surface appears motionless and stable, but scientists believe this thick "crust" is actually made of large plates resting on a fluid layer below the surface. This concept, known as plate tectonics, is the accepted explanation for much of the earth's continuing change geologically.

These plates move constantly, sometimes pressing together and sometimes drifting apart. Although they move only inches per year, when the plates converge, they create immense pressure. Occasionally we see and feel the release of a very small amount of this pressure in earthquakes. The plates' ceaseless movement and pressure helped create and shape the land that became the park.

Scientists surmise that, perhaps 600 million years ago, the North American plate began to break away from the land mass to the east. As the giant plates separated, a rift valley was formed, causing fractures in the Old Rag granite. Then 570 million years ago, lava pushed up through the cracks and fissures of Old Rag. Ash and molten lava emerged to cover what would become the park and hardened to rock. The major plates continued to drift apart, and the Iapetus Ocean covered the area of the park, depositing thousands of feet of sedimentary layers, while Old Rag granite remained deep beneath the earth's surface. The volcanic rock was changed about 450 million years ago when the ocean began to close, causing several small plates to converge with the North American plate. The heat and pressure generated by the plates coming together caused the volcanic ash to metamorphose into purple slate and green phyllite. The lava became greenstone.

Approximately 350 million years ago, the African and North American plates first collided. Then 300 million years ago, the compression caused the crust to buckle and break. In the area of the park, the underlying sedimentary rock, granite, and greenstone pushed through the earth's surface at sharp angles. They thrust over the rocks to the west, creating dramatic peaks like the young mountains of the Alps and Himalayas. This mountain building, or orogeny, continued over millions of years.

Once the stone jutted above the crust, wind, weather, and water wore it down over many more millions of years. The uplifting, warping, and folding of the earth's surface continued, and new rock and stone repeatedly rose and wore away. Old Rag granite broke through and became Old Rag Mountain. Greenstone, too, emerged to form new mountain peaks. These erosion-resistant rocks formed the mountain ridges of the park; the valleys resulted from the erosion of softer limestone.

Millions of years ago, Old Rag and other mountains of the park stood higher than they do today; geologists believe that the mountains reached their maximum height 200 million years ago. While they do not know that maximum height, scientists estimate that at least 30,000 feet of sedimentary rock and additional greenstone wore away to reduce Hawksbill and Stony Man to their present levels. Since uplift and erosion occurred simultaneously, we cannot tell whether these peaks rose only a few feet or many thousand feet above their crests today.

Despite the eons of time and the uncertain processes that produced Old Rag, a climb up the mountain can teach much. The lava that filled the rock's fractures weathers much faster than the granite through which it flowed. This is why straight granite walls remain, while worn-away lava creates a stone stairway. Such stairs are part of the Ridge Trail to Old Rag's summit. Atop the mountain, weathering and cracking are obvious and expected. But something unexpected is also there: solitary, smooth stones, more than ten feet across, rest almost precariously on the mountain's crest. In the Sierra, or New England, these giant stones might be glacial erratics, stones carried and smoothed by the glaciers, then set gently down as the glaciers melted. But the latest ice age did not reach Shenandoah. Wind and water alone have weathered these stones in place, high on the mountaintop.

The park's many waterfalls also testify to its ancient history. Its small area contains sixteen falls more than twenty-five feet high; nine of those fall sixty feet or more. Erosion created cliffs and waterfalls where harder, more resistant rock like granite and greenstone met less-resistant stone. Whiteoak Canyon and its six waterfalls are not only beautiful; they are excellent history texts as well.

The trail to Whiteoak Canyon crosses the Limberlost trail. Another geology lesson waits nearby, a five-foot-tall black rock. This is columnar metabasalt. When lava contracts during cooling, long prisms can form. The prisms may have five, six, or seven sides, ranging in length from several inches to tens of feet. The outlines of these prisms may appear on the stone's surface. As the basalt weathers, the prisms, or "columns," break off, leaving a long, jagged, almost geometric edge. On this black metabasalt beside the trail, both the surface polygon tracings and the columnar edge are visible. Larger examples of such columnar jointing can be found at Franklin Cliffs and Crescent Rock.

Road cuts along the Skyline Drive also reveal geologic history; they laid many concealed layers bare. These cuts and other views along the drive show where the lava flowed, covering certain stones and filling in cracks and fissures of others. The uplift, the folding, and the warping of mountain making are also evident. Science explains this landscape as an interaction between these forces and erosion over millions of years.

But in truth, I cannot grasp the power of these forces and the immense length of time involved. How can we really imagine, much less quantify, the force needed to push miles of sedentary stone up or down to a forty-degree angle? How can we judge, given our own brief life spans, the time wind and water took to carve the smooth stones on Old Rag? I must suspend science's theories and accept these stone mountains as they are. Despite my incomprehension, I marvel at and enjoy each peak, stone, and waterfall. Science tells me their story and their age, but I know them best in my time by touch, sight, and sound.

As the mountains evolved, so did the forests. Ten thousand years ago the most recent ice age neared its end, as the glaciers, 200 miles to the north, retreated. In the valley to the west and the piedmont to the east grew hemlocks, balsam fir, spruce, and gray birch. The mountains were the same size and shape as they are today, but what grew on them is not known with certainty. Evergreen forests may have covered them, or perhaps they were treeless, hosting only alpine flora of small, hardy plants. Long-term work in pollen analysis now under way should tell us more about the vegetation during this period.

As the climate warmed following the last ice age, hemlocks, fir, spruce, and other cold-weather trees moved into the mountains; the striped maple may have been abundant along the base of the Blue Ridge. Over the next several thousand years, the climate grew steadily warmer. Striped maple, fir, gray birch, spruce, and hemlock moved farther up the mountains and also northward. Hemlocks found homes in cool hollows and folds like those along the Rose River and in Whiteoak Canyon.

Today, islands of fir, spruce, striped maple, and similar species grow only in the park's higher reaches. The striped maple appears to thrive at higher elevations and, until recently, so did hemlocks. Several giant hemlocks in Limberlost are estimated to be 350 to 400 years old.

By the arrival of English explorers three centuries ago, the mountains boasted magnificent forests of grand specimens; hardwoods dominated. In the early 1800s, when settlers first arrived, the chestnut was the most common tree in this area, making up 20 to 30 percent of all trees. Black walnut, oak, and poplar were also present.

Shenandoah is unlike most national parks established before it; those preserved undeveloped government land or wilderness areas. European settlers first came to Shenandoah long before 1800. They came to the piedmont and the valley first, then moved up into the hollows and mountains. Although the topsoil was rocky and thin in some areas, it was rich. Those who came to these mountains cleared land and farmed, planted orchards, and raised cattle. Logging and mining companies cut timber and did some shallow mining. These forces changed the land of Shenandoah.

Other changes in Shenandoah have also had human causes. The forest's composition, for example, has shifted dramatically since the early twentieth century. This shift began with the death of the mighty chestnut. In the late 1800s, hybridizers sought to breed a new variety of chestnut that would combine the stately size of the American tree and the larger chestnut of Chinese specimens. The Asian trees they imported, however, carried a deadly fungus. First identified at the New York Zoological Gardens in 1904, this killer blocks the tree's transport of water and nutrients. The chestnut blight traveled fifty miles each year, reaching Shenandoah by the late teens.

Within less than two decades, the chestnut vanished. Chestnuts, once so plentiful in the park, died in place, leaving ranks of pale-gray lifeless trunks, known as ghost forests. The chestnut has never returned. Here and there throughout the park, young sprouts appear, but few mature enough to fruit before the same blight kills them. With the death of the chestnut, the oaks—red oaks, white oaks, and chestnut oaks—took over.

Then, in 1935, the park was established. Not only did the logging and farming stop, but the CCC also planted hundreds of thousands of trees along the drive, in meadows and pastures, and in back-country areas. The CCC also stabilized the land disturbed by the construction of the Skyline Drive. In addition, they removed the dead chestnuts, and some of the wood was used to build the lodge at Big Meadows. With this great help, meadows and orchards gave way to forest.

Now, less than seventy years later, the difference is remarkable. The young trees of the 1940s are maturing; in most places it is difficult to see where the forest of the 1920s and 1930s ends and the newer forest begins. The old mountain roads have taken longer to disappear, but they, too, are dissolving. These positive changes are the result of humankind and nature. The initial assistance of the CCC has been augmented through the years by the continued work of the National Park Service not only with plantings but also with controls and protections to allow nature to function and rejuvenate Shenandoah.

In 1869, at 27 Myrtle Street in Medford, Massachusetts, more than sixty-five years before the park was established, the fertilized eggs of a silk-producing caterpillar brought from France were misplaced. The eggs hatched and the gypsy moth was free where it has no natural enemies. The moth multiplied rapidly, feeding on oaks and other deciduous trees, and moved steadily south along the Appalachians. Gypsy moths reached the northern end of Shenandoah in 1983. Over the next decade the infestation moved along the mountain ridges, affecting more than 100,000 acres, or over half of the park.

Gypsy moth caterpillars can defoliate an entire tree, and oaks are their favorites. Between 80 and 90 percent of trees recover from the first defoliation, but after the second, survival drops to half. After being defoliated three or four times, few trees leaf again. Many decimated oak groves now dot the park, pale trunks of dead trees still standing like the chestnuts before them.

Unlike the chestnut, however, the oak still survives as a species. In fact, oaks in some areas show very little evidence of damage. Elsewhere, however, the gypsy moth has changed the forest again. The moth decimates areas and marches along the mountains for several years, then dies back temporarily. This unwelcome immigrant will continue to play a role in the changing forests of Shenandoah. Poplar, maple, and pine, trees less tasty than the oak, may come to dominate these woods in the future.

As the Ice Age ended, many hemlocks moved from the piedmont and valley to the mountains. Some hemlocks survived ensuing settlement and cultivation, perhaps because of their location. Individuals saved other grand specimens from the loggers' saws, as Addie Pollock did before the park was created.

A hemlock forest is darker and cooler than forests of other species. The trees' thick canopy blocks direct sunlight; their dropped needles are toxic to most other plants. When a hemlock matures, the lower branches die off and nothing grows beneath; the forest floor is clean.

But the hemlock, like the chestnut and the oak, underwent attack by a foreign invader. Although no one knows how, the hemlock woolly adelgid, a tiny airborne insect from Asia discovered in eastern hemlocks in Virginia in the 1950s, was almost certainly imported by humans. The best guess is that the adelgid came in with a shipment of exotic plants to one of Richmond's large estates earlier in the century and wind carried the adelgid to the Blue Ridge.

The woolly adelgid sucks sap from the base of hemlock needles and simultaneously injects a toxic saliva. This causes desiccation and the death of the tree within one to four years. The woolly adelgid arrived at Shenandoah National Park in the mid-1990s and now infests most of the park's hemlocks. While the Park Service has tried spraying to save representative stands of hemlocks, such as Limberlost, many, even in these protected areas, are dead or dying. At Limberlost now, dead hemlocks let in light. Pioneer plants have moved into the small sunny areas, signaling change for these forests, too. Pines, or perhaps surviving oaks, will eventually replace the hemlocks.

POLLUTION OF ALL KINDS is also changing the park. Before the Industrial Revolution overtook the nineteenth century, air and water seemed infinitely self-cleansing. Although localized air pollution eventually became a concern, factories and power plants simply built smokestacks higher and higher so that this self-cleansing air could carry fly ash and other pollutants far from the plant. The air, like the grassy commons of early English villages, became everyone's resource but no one's responsibility. The overburdened air and water became foul and contaminated, spoiling a common benefit.

By the 1960s it was clear that the federal government would have to act to protect our air and water. America recognized, belatedly, that we are one nation, if not one world, ecologically. No matter how high we build smokestacks or how far downstream we dump sewage or chemicals, our private and individual actions not only affect others, but they also affect us.

The park's primary known air pollution problems include acid rain, haze, and ground-level ozone. Sulfur dioxide and nitrogen oxides can transform into acids or airborne particles that impair visibility. These secondary pollutants—particularly sulfur pollutants—can travel hundreds of miles from where they are produced and are key causes of acid rain and man-made haze problems at the park. Recent studies, however, indicate that Virginia and other southeastern and mid-Atlantic states contribute significantly to their own air pollution problems. Preliminary findings from one study indicate that Virginia, Ohio, West Virginia, and Pennsylvania are consistently the top four contributors to sulfur deposition, nitrogen deposition, and sulfate haze impacts at the park. Acid rain has already reduced fish hardiness, populations, and species diversity in several acidified streams in the park. University of Virginia scientists also believe acid rain may weaken plants so that oaks, for example, are more susceptible to insect and disease outbreaks such as gypsy moth.

The first explorers sometimes saw these mountains through a natural bluish haze created by the plants themselves, a haze that gave the Blue Ridge its name. But this haze was evidence of life and growth. At the turn of the twentieth century and into the 1940s, the Shenandoah National Park's views were magnificent. Although Washington lay more than seventy miles northeast, on clear days visitors with telescopes could often see the Washington Monument. Since midcentury, however, the spectacular view from the ridgeline, a major factor in Shenandoah's selection as a national park, and the reason for the Skyline Drive, has dimmed.

A whitish haze clouds the park's summertime horizon. Reddish brown hazes, some of which may be caused by nitrogen pollutants, can also impair the views, especially during the cool seasons. Only a major weather front leaves the views reasonably clear, but they are never completely clear—never the views that moved and astonished George Freeman Pollock. In my experience, truly clear days only occur following a front during October through March, and rarely even then.

Haze is a visible sign of the park's pollution. But some pollution, like ground-level ozone, is invisible but damaging all the same. This "bad ozone" results when volatile organic compounds and nitrogen oxides react together under sunlight. The park has forty known ozone-sensitive plant species and three sensitive forest cover types that dominate almost 80 percent of the park—chestnut oak, poplar, and cove hardwoods.

Hot, sunny, windless days can be ozone factories. Ozone splotches and spots leaves of sensitive species like poplar and milkweed. In Shenandoah National Park, poplar, green ash, sweet gum, black locust, eastern hemlock, Table Mountain pine, and Virginia pine seedlings have all demonstrated growth loss at ozone levels below federal standards to protect human health. Ozone exposures at the park have exceeded limits known to be harmful to sensitive plants for over a decade. Some scientists are now concerned about long-term consequences of ozone exposures on individual plant health and plant ecology.

The EPA's current human safety limit for ozone was exceeded frequently in the park over the last several years of the 1990s. In 1998, for example, ozone levels rose above safe limits twenty-two times. During this period, the late 1990s, "health-based" ozone levels in the park were comparable to those in Richmond and northern Virginia. Under revised, stricter EPA standards, parts of the park, like urban northern Virginia, have been identified as preliminary ozone nonattainment areas, meaning that ozone levels are periodically unhealthy.

The park's location, design, and structure add to its pollution problems. The park is a short drive away for Washingtonians and an easy day trip for millions more. This accessibility is also a curse. "Civilization"—development and industry—surround the park on all sides. Although it is up to thirteen miles wide, in most places the park is six miles wide or less. Further, the Skyline Drive carries tens of thousands of automobiles down the park's backbone every year. Also, two major highways cut through the park. These, combined with the Skyline Drive, divide the park into six parts. In addition to bringing more pollution, roads can be a substantial barrier and danger to wildlife. Snakes and turtles are obvious examples of the threat from automobiles, but the roads' edges affect other animals and plant life as well, making Shenandoah more fragile and difficult to protect.

THE PARK, THEN, is a small island ecosystem that must maintain its equilibrium under assault from inside and outside. A century ago, in *Our National Parks*, John Muir spoke prophetically about the need to protect wild places and about government's role in that protection:

> Any fool can destroy trees. They cannot run away; and if they could, they would still be destroyed,—chased and hunted down as long as fun or a dollar could be got out of their bark hides, branching horns, or magnificent bole backbones. . . . Through all the wonderful, eventful centuries since Christ's time—and long before that—God has cared for these trees, saved them from drought, disease, avalanches, and a thousand straining, leveling tempests and floods; but he cannot save them from fools,—only Uncle Sam can do that. (364-65)

When Muir wrote, ancient forests were in danger from loggers. Today, the menace is more pervasive and more insidious. The ax and saw are not the greatest threat now—we are. All of us. All of us who drive cars, use electricity, and participate in our disposable society, even those of us who most appreciate the wonders of Shenandoah and other untamed places.

We live in a complex and prosperous society. That society's by-products threaten the very existence of parks and other wild places. Muir's words, written a century ago are more ominous and prophetic today when we look at places like Shenandoah. Trees, like humans and other animals, need good soil, good water, and good air to thrive.

Although any discussion of Shenandoah National Park must speak of encroaching pollution and the need for protection and preservation, I write to warn and encourage, not to keep new visitors away. Shenandoah's vulnerabilities emphasize the problems and pollution outside the park as well, the problems and pollution we, too, live with but may not notice in our daily lives.

As a nation, America spent its first 300 years conquering nature; only in the last century have we become protectors of wildness and natural areas. Our efforts in the first half of the twentieth century primarily involved stopping the ax and saw in order to save or create places like Shenandoah. By the middle of the twentieth century, we realized that air and water need protection as much as forests and wildlife. In the 1960s and 1970s, we began that work of preservation and restoration. The Clean Air Act of 1990 and its amendments aimed to reduce sulfur dioxide and by the late 1990s brought tangible results. These benefits at the park and other areas, however, will likely be reduced if revised projections of increased sulfur dioxide emissions under Phase II of the Acid Rain program in Virginia come to pass.

We have also identified and protected endangered species of plants and animals and have specified and preserved wilderness areas. Although much work remains and new pollutants will undoubtedly appear, America has committed herself in spirit and theory, if not always in fact, to protecting places like Shenandoah. Such protection remains an evolving and still incomplete process.

Shenandoah's special needs, and those of wilderness and wildness, are important. But Shenandoah is indeed the refuge it was meant to be, a protected, special, and beautiful place. The air is cool, and the vistas can be spectacular and beautiful. The columbine and wild geranium bloom and grow, the ferns push aside last year's leaves, vigorous evidence of renewal. The water that flows over the six falls in Whiteoak Canyon shines and sprays as magnificently as it did a thousand years ago. The smooth stones on Old Rag that made the Native Americans wonder are still cause for wonder.

The fawns, now born every year at the edges of Big Meadows just as they were before settlers came, can populate the park for centuries to come. The woods are quiet; the birds call at dawn. You will still be startled by the flashing bright yellow of goldfinches in flight.

John Muir urged us to "climb the mountains and get their good tidings." Do this at Shenandoah. Enjoy the views from the overlooks, but be sure to walk, too. Leave your car behind, explore the trails, and pause beside the quiet pools, cascades, and falls. Study the streams, the rocks, the clouds, a single tree in sunlight, a new fern, or a solitary leaf.

Leave your notebook and laptop, too. Go not to count or categorize flora and fauna. Go to be one with nature. Join nature, or rejoin it. Drink in the peace and solitude. Go, and listen, and watch, with your spirit as well as your senses. Come into the park and let it come into you. Then you will understand why we must preserve and protect its beautiful wildness. Your first trip to Shenandoah will be one of many; you will know that John Muir was right:

> Climb the mountains and get their good tidings. Nature's peace will flow into you as sunshine flows into trees. The winds will blow their own freshness into you, and the storms their energy, while cares will drop off like autumn leaves. (56)

FURTHER READING

Badger, Robert L. *Geology along Skyline Drive*. Helena, Mont.: Falcon Publishing, 1999.

Crandall, Hugh, and Reed Engle. *Shenandoah: The Story behind the Scenery*. Las Vegas: KC Publications. Revised edition, 1997.

Engle, Reed L. *Everything Was Wonderful: A Pictorial History of the Civilian Conservation Corps in Shenandoah National Park*. Luray, Va.: Shenandoah Natural History Association (now Shenandoah National Park Association), 1999.

Floyd, Tom. *Lost Trails and Forgotten People*. Vienna, Va.: Potomac Appalachian Trail Club, 1981.

Lambert, Darwin. *Herbert Hoover's Hideaway*. Luray, Va.: Shenandoah Natural History Association (now Shenandoah National Park Association), 1971.

———. *The Undying Past of Shenandoah National Park*. Boulder, Colo.: Roberts Rinehart (in cooperation with Shenandoah Natural History Association, now Shenandoah National Park Association), 1989.

Muir, John. *Our National Parks*. Boston: Houghton Mifflin, 1901.

Reeder, Carolyn, and Jack Reeder. *Shenandoah Secrets: The Story of the Park's Hidden Past*. Vienna, Va.: Potomac Appalachian Trail Club, 1991.

Photographer's Notes

I have been visiting the Shenandoah National Park since the mid-sixties. I have walked many, if not most, of the trails and visited the waterfalls. I have come in every season, most often enjoying this special place alone. While I made a number of photographs in the early years, I did not begin photographing in the park seriously until 1980.

For Christmas in 1979, my wife gave me a Calumet 4×5–inch monorail view camera and the toys that went with it. She also gave me ten days in Yosemite National Park at a workshop with Ansel Adams. It was glorious. For ten days, along with sixty others, I ate, drank, breathed, and lived photography at Yosemite.

We listened and watched Ansel as he talked and demonstrated his life's work. In addition to Ansel, other notable photographers worked with us every day. I was immersed. I found my avocation.

One of those working with Ansel that summer was his young assistant, John Sexton. John was far more than an assistant; he is now a deservedly celebrated photographer in his own right and the finest printmaker in the country, if not the world. He, like Ansel before him, shares his knowledge. I have been fortunate over the years to attend two of John's workshops.

In 1980 I came to the Shenandoah National Park with a vision to capture, in part, what I see and feel here. The pictures in this book were made between August of 1981 and May of 2002. They represent thousands of hours in the park and darkroom and almost as many driving. I have made exposures in every part of the park. Some places were easy, with the first or second trip capturing what I saw. Other places remain elusive, images I see but am not yet able to capture. The photographs here are a small portion of those I have made in Shenandoah. I still remember Ansel saying, "You are not judged by the pictures you make, only those you show." I hope I have chosen well.

I remember making every image in this book; I can close my eyes and relive the moment. Unfortunately, especially for some early pictures, I did not note the date and, for a few, I cannot identify the exact location. All photographs were made in the park except *Apple Blossoms and Old Rag*, which is a view of Old Rag Mountain from an apple orchard near the park. I have estimated dates when I did not have complete notes.

All of the photographs in this book were made with a 4 × 5–inch view camera. The Calumet monorail was heavy and cumbersome, barely suited to carry in town, much less down the trails of Shenandoah. My second camera was a lightweight wooden field view camera that was destroyed when a hiker above me dislodged a rock that knocked the camera, but not me, off the ledge I was perched on; I still have the pieces recovered from 75 feet below. Since then I have used a Zone VI 4 × 5–inch view camera. With a few exceptions I have relied on Kodak film. The earlier photographs were made with Kodak Tri-X Professional Film, with HC110 developer at various dilutions. Beginning in the late 1980s, I shifted to T-Max, most often T-Max 100, developed in T-Max developer, again, at various dilutions.

The prints were made using a variety of graded and variable contrast paper. Many, especially the recent prints, were made on Forte V variable contrast, fiber-based, double-weight, glossy paper developed in Factor One developer diluted 1:15. Almost all prints required some form of burning or dodging, and I used a mask on several prints.

Information about the negatives of the images in this book follows. Where information was not available, I have made estimates.

TECHNICAL INFORMATION

Frontispiece
Appalachian Trail and Mist
LOCATION: Appalachian Trail
near milepost 92.5, Skyline
Drive
DATE: October 2, 1994
FILM: T-Max 100
LENS: 210 mm
EXPOSURE: f/22⅔, 10 secs.
DEVELOPMENT: N

12
*Baldface Mountain Overlook,
1981*
LOCATION: Baldface Moun-
tain Overlook
DATE: August 1981
FILM: Tri-X
LENS: 210 mm
EXPOSURE: f/32⅓, 1/30 sec.;
Filter No. 15
DEVELOPMENT: N

13
*Baldface Mountain Overlook,
1988*
LOCATION: Baldface Moun-
tain Overlook
DATE: November 12, 1988
FILM: Tri-X
LENS: 210 mm
EXPOSURE: f/32, ½ sec.; Filter
No. 25
DEVELOPMENT: N

14
Stony Man Mountain
LOCATION: Skyline Drive
near Stony Man Mountain
DATE: May 21, 1995;
8:45 A.M.
FILM: T-Max 100
LENS: 210 mm
EXPOSURE: f/22½, ¼ sec.;
Filter No. 8
DEVELOPMENT: N

15
Dogwoods
DATE: April 15, 1995;
6:00 P.M.
FILM: T-Max 100
LENS: 210 mm
EXPOSURE: f/32, ½ sec.
DEVELOPMENT: N

16
Bloodroot at Sugar Hollow
LOCATION: Sugar Hollow
DATE: April 10, 1994
FILM: T-Max 100
LENS: 210 mm
EXPOSURE: f/45, 4 secs.
DEVELOPMENT: N−1

17
New Ferns
LOCATION: Roadside, Skyline
Drive
DATE: May 16, 1992
FILM: T-Max 400
LENS: 210 mm
EXPOSURE: f/45, 5 secs.
DEVELOPMENT: N−1

18
Doyles River Falls
LOCATION: Doyles River Falls
DATE: April 1983
FILM: Tri-X
LENS: 210 mm
EXPOSURE: f/32½, 1 sec.
DEVELOPMENT: N−2

19
Little Fall and Fern
LOCATION: Hogcamp Branch,
near Dark Hollow Falls
DATE: June 24, 1990
FILM: T-Max 400
LENS: 210 mm
EXPOSURE: f/32½, 1 sec.
DEVELOPMENT: N

Negatives were exposed and developed using the "Zone System." Accordingly, exposure and development were varied to change contrast. "N" refers to development time. N = normal development
to yield normal contrast. N−1 = decrease in development time to reduce contrast by approximately
one zone. N−2 = decrease in development time to reduce contrast by approximately two zones. N+1
= increase in development time to increase contrast by approximately one zone. N+2 = increase in
development time to increase contrast by approximately two zones.

20

Rose River Falls, High Water

LOCATION: Rose River Falls

DATE: September 9, 2000;
    12:30 P.M.

FILM: T-Max 100

LENS: 120 mm

EXPOSURE: f/16⅔, 1 sec.

DEVELOPMENT: N−1

21

Dancing Dogwoods

LOCATION: Entrance, South
    River Picnic Area

DATE: August 28, 1997;
    1:00 P.M.

FILM: T-Max 100

LENS: 355 mm

EXPOSURE: f/16, ⅟₁₅ sec.

DEVELOPMENT: N

23

Mountain Stream

LOCATION: Sugar Hollow

DATE: May 3, 1996; 7:45 P.M.

FILM: T-Max 100

LENS: 210 mm

EXPOSURE: f/32⅔, 25 secs.

DEVELOPMENT: N+2

24

Apple Blossoms and Old Rag

LOCATION: Apple orchard
    near Virginia State Route
    644

DATE: April 22, 1995;
    9:00 A.M.

FILM: T-Max 100

LENS: 210 mm

EXPOSURE: f/32, ¼ sec.; Filter
    No. 8

DEVELOPMENT: N

25

Service Berry and Dogwood

LOCATION: Near entrance
    station, Swift Run Gap

DATE: April 25, 1999;
    8:30 A.M.

FILM: T-Max 100

LENS: 355 mm

EXPOSURE: f/11, ⅟₁₅ sec.

DEVELOPMENT: N

26

Old Rag Mountain

LOCATION: Thorofare Moun-
    tain Overlook

DATE: April 18, 1982

FILM: Tri-X

LENS: 210 mm

EXPOSURE: f/32½, ½ sec.;
    Filter No. 8

DEVELOPMENT: N

27

Young Ferns and Oaks

LOCATION: Near Skyline
    Drive, North Section

DATE: May 27, 2000;
    10:00 A.M.

FILM: T-Max 100

LENS: 210 mm

EXPOSURE: f/32⅔, 5 secs.

DEVELOPMENT: N

28

Hogcamp Branch

LOCATION: Hogcamp Branch,
    below fire road

DATE: October 1987

FILM: Tri-X

LENS: 210 mm

EXPOSURE: f/45, 40 secs.

DEVELOPMENT: N

29

Whiteoak Falls

LOCATION: Whiteoak Falls

DATE: April 18, 1982

FILM: Tri-X

LENS: 120 mm

EXPOSURE: f/45, 1 sec., Filter
    No. 25

DEVELOPMENT: N−2

30

Mayapples, Rain

LOCATION: Roadside, Skyline
    Drive

DATE: April 1996

FILM: T-Max 100

LENS: 210 mm

EXPOSURE: f/45, 15 sec.

DEVELOPMENT: N

31

False Hellebore

LOCATION: Near Naked Creek
    Overlook

DATE: April 18, 1998;
    10:15 A.M.

FILM: T-Max 100

LENS: 210 mm

EXPOSURE: f/45, 11 sec.

DEVELOPMENT: N

32

Frozen at Naked Creek

LOCATION: Naked Creek Falls

DATE: January 27, 1991

FILM: T-Max 400

LENS: 210 mm

EXPOSURE: f/32½, 1 sec.

DEVELOPMENT: N

33

Ice Orb and Lace

LOCATION: Naked Creek

DATE: January 27, 1991

FILM: T-Max 400

LENS: 210 mm

EXPOSURE: f/45, 1 sec.

DEVELOPMENT: N

34

Downstream, Moormans River

LOCATION: North Fork of
    Moormans River

DATE: May 25, 1997;
    10:00 A.M.

FILM: T-Max 100

LENS: 355 mm

EXPOSURE: f/64⅔, 4 secs.;
    Filter, ND.6

DEVELOPMENT: N

35

Cold Heart, Hogcamp Branch

LOCATION: Hogcamp Branch

DATE: February 1, 1997;
    12:25 P.M.

FILM: T-Max 100

LENS: 355 mm

EXPOSURE: f/64⅔, 5 secs.

DEVELOPMENT: N

36

Horse Pot

LOCATION: Cabin ruins

DATE: October 12, 1996;
    1:05 P.M.

FILM: T-Max 100

LENS: 210 mm

EXPOSURE: f/45, 15 secs.

DEVELOPMENT: N

37
Silver Leaf
LOCATION: Sugar Hollow
DATE: November 16, 1992
FILM: T-Max 100
LENS: 210 mm
EXPOSURE: f/45, 12 secs.
DEVELOPMENT: N

38
Mountain Clouds
LOCATION: Sandy Bottom
    Overlook
DATE: August 14, 1999;
    2:35 P.M.
FILM: T-Max 100
LENS: 210 mm
EXPOSURE: f/22, ⅟₁₅ sec.;
    Filter No. 12
DEVELOPMENT: N

39
Big Meadows Oak,
    Summer Clouds
LOCATION: Big Meadows
DATE: August 14, 1999;
    3:30 P.M.
FILM: T-Max 100
LENS: 210 mm
EXPOSURE: f/16, ⅟₃₀ sec.;
    Filter No. 12
DEVELOPMENT: N

41
Moormans River, Sugar
    Hollow, Spring
LOCATION: North Fork of
    Moormans River
DATE: May 20, 1995; 7:30 P.M.
FILM: T-Max 100
LENS: 210 mm
EXPOSURE: f/32½, 48 secs.
DEVELOPMENT: N

42
Board Detail, Cabin Remains
DATE: October 12, 1996;
    1:20 P.M.
FILM: T-Max 100
LENS: 210 mm
EXPOSURE: f/16⅔, 1 sec.
DEVELOPMENT: N

43
Seeds
LOCATION: Near Skyline
    Drive
DATE: December 1990
FILM: T-Max 400
LENS: 210 mm
EXPOSURE: Unknown
DEVELOPMENT: Unknown

44
Dark Hollow Falls
LOCATION: Upper Dark
    Hollow Falls
DATE: June 20, 1982
FILM: Tri-X
LENS: 210 mm
EXPOSURE: f/45, 1 sec.
DEVELOPMENT: N–1

45
Flood Tree Remains,
    Moormans River
LOCATION: North Fork of
    Moormans River
DATE: October 13, 1996;
    6:00 P.M.
FILM: T-Max 100
LENS: 210 mm
EXPOSURE: f/45, 5 sec.
DEVELOPMENT: N

46
Flame Cloud
LOCATION: Skyline Drive
DATE: November 12, 1988
FILM: Tri-X
LENS: 210 mm
EXPOSURE: f/32, ⅟₃₀ sec.;
    Filter No. 15
DEVELOPMENT: N

47
Skyline Vista
LOCATION: Skyline Drive
DATE: November 1988
FILM: Tri-X
LENS: 210 MM
EXPOSURE: Unknown, Filter
    No. 15
DEVELOPMENT: Unknown

48
Forest Floor, Limberlost
LOCATION: Limberlost Forest
DATE: December 1990
FILM: Tri-X
LENS: 210 mm
EXPOSURE: f/45, 1 sec.
DEVELOPMENT: N

49
Big Meadows Branch
    and Grass
LOCATION: Big Meadows
DATE: September 1990
FILM: T-Max 400
LENS: 210 mm
EXPOSURE: f/45, 1 sec.
DEVELOPMENT: N

50
Big Meadows Oak,
    Spring Frost
LOCATION: Big Meadows
DATE: March 30, 1991
FILM: T-Max 400
LENS: 210 mm
EXPOSURE: f/45, ⅟₃₀ sec.;
    Filter No. 15
DEVELOPMENT: N

51
South River Falls
LOCATION: South River Falls
DATE: May 24, 1987
FILM: Tri-X
LENS: 120 mm
EXPOSURE: f/32½, 1 sec.
DEVELOPMENT: N

53
Old Rag Boulder and View
LOCATION: Old Rag summit
DATE: January 1, 2001;
    12:25 P.M.
FILM: T-Max 100
LENS: 120 mm
EXPOSURE: f/32⅔, ½ sec.;
    Filter No. 23A
DEVELOPMENT: N

54
Lewis Falls
LOCATION: Lewis Falls
DATE: October 1987
FILM: Tri-X
LENS: 210 mm
EXPOSURE: f/32, 1 sec.
DEVELOPMENT: N

55
Chimney, October Light
DATE: October 23, 1999;
11:00 A.M.
FILM: T-Max 100
LENS: 120 mm
EXPOSURE: f/16⅔, 1 sec;
Filter No. 15
DEVELOPMENT: N

56
Moormans River, Winter
LOCATION: North Fork of
Moormans River
DATE: January 29, 1995
FILM: T-Max 100
LENS: 210 mm
EXPOSURE: f/45, 5 secs.;
Filter No. 8
DEVELOPMENT: N

57
Overall Run Falls
LOCATION: Overall Run Falls
DATE: May 30, 2002; 5:40 P.M.
FILM: T-Max 100
LENS: 210 mm
EXPOSURE: f/32, 1 sec.
DEVELOPMENT: N

58
Ribbon of Whiteoak
LOCATION: Whiteoak Falls
DATE: April 18, 1982
FILM: Tri-X
LENS: 210 mm
EXPOSURE: f/45, 3 secs.;
Filter No. 15
DEVELOPMENT: N–2

59
*Big Meadows Pine, Fog
and Ice*
LOCATION: Big Meadows
DATE: March 30, 1991
FILM: T-Max 400
LENS: 210 mm
EXPOSURE: f/16½, ⅟₁₂₅ sec.
DEVELOPMENT: N

60
Ghost Trees
LOCATION: Skyline Drive,
near milepost 92
DATE: October 6, 1996;
9:35 A.M.
FILM: T-Max 100
LENS: 355 mm
EXPOSURE: f/32⅓, ½ sec.
DEVELOPMENT: N

61
Ivy Creek Overlook, Clouds
LOCATION: Ivy Creek Over-
look
DATE: December 22, 1990
FILM: T-Max 400
LENS: 210 mm
EXPOSURE: f/32, ½ sec.
DEVELOPMENT: N

62
Rest in Peace
LOCATION: Cave family
cemetery
DATE: April 16, 2000;
11:35 A.M.
FILM: T-Max 100
LENS: 210 mm
EXPOSURE: f/16⅔, ⅛ sec.
DEVELOPMENT: N

63
Cave Family Cemetery
LOCATION: Cave family
cemetery
DATE: April 16, 2000;
12:20 P.M.
FILM: T-Max 100
LENS: 210 mm
EXPOSURE: f/32⅔, ½ sec.;
Filter No. 23A
DEVELOPMENT: N

65
Winter Frost, Skyline Drive
LOCATION: Skyline Drive,
milepost 82
DATE: November 26, 1993
FILM: T-Max 100
LENS: 210 mm
EXPOSURE: f/45, ⅟₃₀ sec.
DEVELOPMENT: N

Acknowledgments

This book began in the early 1980s as an idea and a box with the word *book* on the outside and several prints inside. Since then, numerous prints have moved in and out of the box. Many people have helped the idea and box become this book. I thank them all, some of whom I mention here.

Park personnel from superintendents Wade and Morris to rangers such as Barb Stewart and many others protect and defend this special place and assist all of us who visit the park. Other members of the staff used their expertise to review my essays to ensure accuracy. These include Sally Hurlbert, Christi Gordon, Reed Engle, Joanne Amberson, Mara Meisel, Gordon Olson, and Claire Comer.

Ansel Adams remains an inspiration, and his photographs are a constant reminder of what can be done with light and silver. John Sexton has provided help and encouragement through his seminars and advice and, by example, leadership to all of us who make pictures.

Linda Lacy and Toni OBrion, accomplished artists in their own right, helped select images from the box and arrange their order for this book.

Greta Miller of the Shenandoah National Park Association took a chance and carried my posters beginning in 1990. Roy Carter of Gallery 5800 in Richmond, Virginia, also took a chance and gave me my first one-man show. Mark Miller of Suitable for Framing, also in Richmond, mounts and mats all of my prints; he makes everything look good.

Finally, I thank my family. My children, Frank and Sara, put up with many long stops in the park to make a picture. They were patient and have provided much encouragement. And, most of all, I thank my wife, Nancy, who has stayed the course with me.

Designed by Glen Burris, set by the designer in Monotype Bell, and printed on 140-gsm Japanese Matte Art at C & C Offset Printing Company Limited.

A deluxe limited edition of 425 signed and numbered copies was also printed and bound with a slipcase. Four hundred are accompanied by one original photographic print, and twenty-five are accompanied by four original photographic prints.